John L ....

by Louise Warren
Illustrated by John Duffin

V.

Published in the United Kingdom in 2019
by V. Press,
10 Vernon Grove,
Droitwich,
Worcestershire,
WR9 9LQ.

ISBN: 978-1-9165052-8-5

Printed in the U. K. by Vernon Print & Design, Droitwich, WR9 8QZ.

Acknowledgments

To my son William.

*'The Marshes' won first prize Prole Laureate Competition 2018 and a version of 'Town'
(entitled 'He come up for the day') was highly commended in Brittle Star Poetry
Competition 2018. The following poems were first/previously published by the
following journals: Cuckoo in The Lonely Crowd; 'Contoured Map of Exmoor
Popular Edition' in Dream Catcher; John Dust and Woman with small dog (Bumping
into a neighbor) in Strix; Owl Strike in The Lake; Winter Bathroom and Piano in New
Welsh Review 2016 (and also as two short films in collaboration with Cardiff School of
Art).*

V.

Contents

V.

V.

John Dust

pushes through hedgerow
caved in, busted.
John Dust
narrow as a pipe, face like a clay bowl
choked-up, stony-broke
chest blown open like a sunset.
John Dust
face like a field turned over
face full of buttercups, open
face full of cows like a nursery rhyme
nothing but ringing, rusting on bell ropes
nothing but walking
nothing but soaking, clouds like a snot cloth
clouds like a milk slop
lace in his pockets
snot on the hedgerows.
John Dust
face like a millstone, coat stuffed with apples
coat stuffed with horsehair, tied round with sail rope
coat bursting open, burst out the linings
sodden green ditches, pricked through with heron
pierced through with willow, bloody and wasted.
John Dust
face like a battle, like a lane leaking water
passed out in an orchard
fetched from the market, fetched from the weather vane
fetched by the others, smarmy as badgers
pissed up and laughing, waxy as moonshine
stuck in the river mud, turning his pockets out
singing a cuckoo, singing a gatepost
singing an easterly, singing a teasel bed.

John Dust
shut your mouth now
shut it with bell ropes, shut it with horse hair
shut it with bitter cress, teasel and buttercup
shut it with paper, shut it with rifles
shut it with apples, shut it with water
stopped in the ditches.
John Dust
stands up again, face like a neighbour.

The Marshes

In the barn, my sofa stands in its puff of white breath,
heavy, patient, packed in tight with the herd,
waiting. I wait for it.

Downstairs, the afternoon moves heavily around the house,
a washing line turns slowly on its stalk,
the carpet in the hallway runs a sluggish ditch.

Back then, before they built on it, back then
the path stumped short into nettles, just fields,
arm of the sky bent round, empty.

Empty as pockets, empty as churches,
empty as milk pails rusting on gateposts.
I look out the windows milky with flat screens,

empty as ditches,
cold in the kitchen, biting like nettles,
sheeny as hoar frost.

Deep inside the bathroom I undress myself for you,
John Dust.
Down to the sedge and water, down to the beak of me,

sharp in the reed bed, down to the hidden.
I strip the light from my skin until I am overcast,
become cloud cover.

John Dust.
My man under the motorway,
flat out in the dark fields, seeding the hedges,

scratching your chest hair, wispy as larches,
pinking like evening, stitchwort and abattoir, bloody as Sedgemoor,
lipped up with cider, scraggy as winter.

You fetch each room, one by one, back to the marshes.
Plant forks and teaspoons, chairs for the heron's nest,
propped up and broken,

the sky rusting over, smashed up with egg yolks,
water as mirror, water as leather, water as smoke, as trick,
a light under the door.

I stand in the empty
waiting for nothing.
Birds in the buckthorn, a house full of berries.

Cuckoo

Behind the door, he hangs his tongue on a nail
but I can hear the whirring of trapped wings.

In that space between one minute and the next
my imposter waits, in the scratchy dark,

a room that smells of rust; he inhabits it like a stifled cough.
Listen, he is straining every wired nerve.

It is time – for the hands to jump one on top of the other;
it is all for this, the strike and the door opening.

Don't look. He knows he is disappointing;
we are both disappointed.

It's not real I want to say but that isn't the point.

Owl Strike

That night the owl printed a ghost of an owl
as it slammed into the window
the moon held its breath
a frozen

oh

but I did not cry out
burrowing deeper into the leaves
I was not caught by the owl's metal hooks

that night I was safe from harm
from his sudden yellow glare.
He spied my small bones wrapped up in the bedroom dark
but the window stopped him –

he spilt his white heat onto the glass
the night rushed in, all the stars
blazed and froze inside that tiny skull

then flung him back off kilter
sped him somewhere other.
I searched for the smallest feather
found nothing.

Woman with small dog

visiting the museum with John Dust

You said 'I know her
lit up now in a glass box
little dog beside her
bones licked clean on the bottom shelf
cold as the pantry come winter
shovelled in deeper than heartbreak
footsteps swept clean by green brushes
laid down like apples to last
watched by a rook in the wire of a tree
as the night took the moon by the throat
dangled it over the river
tucked her in tight
worms soft as salve
look at her
no more chatter on
tongue eased up from its cradle
skull tipped back for the final rinse
ribs like a purse pulled open
legs bent this way, rusted as hairpins
what a thing
no more queuing, no more dragging
no more ailing, no more rooting –
is this what we come to?
Thought that I knew her
passing along now, excuse me just passing.'

In the Museum of Somerset there is a skeleton of a woman with a dog. 300-400 AD.
Found in Ilchester, Somerset.

The Drowned Field

Something like a man in there,
face down, coat spilled open.

Something like a cow in there,
something like a sheep in there,
something like a cloud in there, floating.

A man, a cow, a sheep, a cloud,
something like a song in there, clear across the water.

A woman singing, clear,
a man singing in the reeds.

A child, a reed, a bird in there,
wings spread open.

Brown bird, brown water,
something like a glass in there,
something like the sea in there, shining.

A man, a bird, a song, a cloud,
a woman singing clear across the water.

A cow, a sheep, a child, a reed
something like a field in there, drowning.

Winter Bathroom

Out of the tap runs a long cold evening, the colour of lead,
of November between the hours of four and six;
I am at the locked door,
the frozen dark

where mirrors are upended and I
am suspended above these gleaming puddles
seeing nothing, only a clouding over
a drained sky

as I wash my face in the sudden rush of night.
I do not know myself, that startled bird
flying out of my eye, sodden glitter to the trees'
empty socket.

Hear my smallest sound, the swallowed cry;
smell my foxes' stink. On all fours
catch the scruff of my ruined fur
as I lie low this long wet night.

Piano

Someone playing a piano in the middle of the forest.
Small flecks fall from the beech trees, dissolve and fade;
the same notes picked out again between the ivory trunks.

Pinpricks of light turning around and around in the wooden box.
Dark inside, a dry Victorian smell, and fragments of burnt paper
have blown out and gathered at my feet like leaves.

When I pull away, the forest is silent and my fingertips are bruised green.
All the trees look the same to me, one chord following another,
the path has vanished, a pile of logs like tightly rolled manuscripts

or wax cylinders. Maybe one day someone will burn it onto a disc.
The sun flashing though splinters and shadows, my footsteps stick
onto a soft black mush, crushed needles, as I try and wind myself backwards

Swifts

John Dust, you were with me at dawn,
great pale feet stuck out the caravan door.
Tucked in, a skinned hare, turned milk, tinned meat,
a sink full of onion skin and hair.

Weather, full of it, wetter,
you turned a spell of it out the one tap,
slid up me like wet grass, wetter,
The late sun, redder and redder.

'Wear it like your face' you said, laughing,
climbing over me like a stile,
like the smell of gorse, sudden and hot,
'I will be your Silhouette, your Diplomat, your Compass.'

The rooks rise up, could I settle here?
A bed no wider than a grave,
the table with its broken leg, buying my one egg,
you waiting, jamming up the bog.

'There is always a caravan' you say,
'always one buried in the wood,
seams broke up and rich with rust,
a dulled yellow window bulged out like a blister.'

You follow me up the road,
stuck on like a burr.
'I will be your Swift' you say,
'the rest is birdshit and singsong.'

Silhouette, Diplomat, Compass and Swift are all caravans.

Fly

How beautiful and delicate he is in death
laid out on the white afterlife
like a god, a fly on the sill
in a tapestry of cup rings.

His perfect crossed legs, tiny fanned wings
his carbon black body.
I file past him in the kitchen of all things –
the universe holds its breath behind invisible ropes.

East Coker

'*Willow, Laurel.*'
You chant it like a prayer under your muddy breath.
The bus spins round, at every turn another crop of houses.
'*Maple, Beech, Rowan, Lime.*'

Set me down at *Coker*,
set me down at *Tallis Cross*, at the *Hang Gate*, at the *Hall*.
lead me to *East Coker*, up the lane to *East Coker*.
The bus spins round, the clock strikes twelve.

The lane absorbs me in its heat.
Intense yellow flowers spill from ditches,
yellow the lichen on the wall,
intense the smell from the yellow flowers.

Inside the empty church the cold air waits
as a pond waits in a field,
with cattle drinking or lain down in the heat.
The clock strikes one.

The bus spins round, you call it like a poem.
'*Willow, Laurel, Maple, Beech, Rowan, Lime,*
Tallis Cross, the *Hang Gate*, and the *Hall*,
I shall lead you to *East Coker*, up the lane to *East Coker*.'

Town

You tried to come up for the day.
Come up by coach, by train, come up by Jack the Treacle Eater
flying out his folly.

Come up by your own thin legs, striking over Ash Lane,
field and sluice gate, yard, the slimed canal,
then two miles on you turned.

Turned again, then turned back,
heel caught in a rut, in the gnawed hock of an old moon,
caught in a bramble snare, a fist of frost,

a rain so light and fine it wrapped you up like hair.
Up you tripped into next door's dog, into drizzle, dusk,
the Ring of Bells, tripped up on love,

on longing for it. Couldn't run to save your life.
Tried to turn, but turned so many times
you spun, spun to a fir cone, your brown coat wrapped round tight.

Six coats, ten, fifty, maybe more, a lifetime, more;
you felt your father, uncle, neighbour, man who brought the eggs,
coats that smelt of wax, of blood and straw.

Still you turned: the coach had gone,
Jack the Treacle Eater rusted in a field, you'd missed the train,
lay down in a nettle bed and felt a fool.

A year went by and still you lay,
those coats of brown grew brittle, and the bright

shrill narrow light that fell into the ditch was just the same.

A sword, a wand, a tractor's stare,
it woke you, and you swore, and made for home.

Jack the Treacle Eater is one of four follies in Barwick, Somerset. A small winged figure on top of a steeple, the story goes that Jack ran messages from Barwick to London and kept fit on a diet of treacle.

The Parish Magazine

Item 1. Cricket Fixtures

Ernest Shilling bowled his last before expiring in a pharmaceutical haze. All eyes were on the ball which spun in a perfect curve over the heads of the fielders and landed in another universe beyond the green. A vast domed planet, frozen and sealed in layers of slithering plastic. The sphere of burnished leather became in that barren land, an image of a new dawn. So we pass over that particular cornerstone of history and back to the game which was halted for a short break while the ambulance was called. Tea was served in the small pavilion, a small crowd gathered around the chilling body. A tea towel placed over the face, featuring cuts of meat in vivid shades of red and pink. Something from the village gift shop, Local Trades. Then in smaller letters Spiller and Son Butchers 1922-1988. Also passed away.

Item 2. A nasty incident in the village Shop

It was while her back was turned that Mrs. Finch was disturbed by the intruder who entered the crepuscular aisles of the back passage and escaped with a packet of Earl Grey tea and a pasty (both thankfully past their sell by date). Mrs. Finch immediately evacuated the premises which was empty at the time apart from herself and a small immobile child, long dead and forgotten since the closure of the primary school in 1991.

Item 3. Fouling on the Village Green

The night has that 1970s' retro feel. Velvety green grass, below a flocked and disco-lit starry sky, trees cast long skinny shadows, flaring out at the hems. Nothing to do but hang off the swings. Sixteen and pissed on cider, they prickle with acne and nettles, legs going numb on the rotten planks. They run off laughing, the commemorative bench gets a good kicking, their shadows spoil the pond like poison.

Item 4. Neighbourhood Watch

She stood for several hours in the leylandii hedge, picking broken teeth out of her slippers. One by one the lights went out in the bungalow, the metal grills lowered, the electric force field activated, soon the place was a sinister oblong humming gently in the dusk. *Danger! Death!* read the sign above the door, lovingly hand-painted with tendrils of honeysuckle and roses. She made her move; static played havoc with her nylon nighty but her eyeball made contact with the keyhole. Slick as a gooseberry it squished further in, bubbled out at the end and plopped onto the mat. Soon all would be revealed.

Item 5. A Celebration in Music

On their backs in the crackling frost, hatless, a chorus of pensioners listening for the first thrust of early rhubarb. A low fat moon glimmers weakly overhead, fuzzy from the incoming wash of light pollution. Illuminated dimly, an elderly man clasped to an ancient apple tree, waiting for those tender little gas jets to spurt into life. He reaches up into the veins of the branches, humming along to *Lord Lamborne, Tom Putt, Lady Sudely.* His wife buries her head in a clump of unripe primroses, coaxing a breathless thread of song from those pinkly frozen stems. *All together now, as one clear voice. Spring is upon us, let us rejoice!*

Contoured Road Map of Exmoor. Popular Edition.

Folded in on itself, the texture of lining, gabardine –
an expanding pocket, empty, miles of it

opening and opening –
laid flat the folds are stained brown like rust

or from a distance wet bracken – blasted, thin wiry hedges –
some kind of bird is trapped here, flapping and panicking –

some kind of weather is trapped here – damping, a cloud
from the 30s, pressed onto the page – vapour thin fog expanding –

some kind of man is trapped here – his back to me smoking –

5 riddles

1.

Never runs, stops.

Swallows a moon, swallows a cow
swallows the light like a sword
swallows you drunk.

Trips you up
crosses you.
Belches, bubbles, sucks at straws
swells, swallows a road, a field, a sky
slinks back, hides, a zipped-up fly.

John Dust knows it like the back of his hand.
Flat. Like the palm of his hand.
Crossing. Criss-crossed.

2.

We swing towards the bend
then stop just short
we're end to end.

We wait in line
our metal armour glitters in the heat
our magnets pull towards the sign.

He calls us from the hills,
the muddied coast
come to my Swift! My Pearl! My Compass!

As either side, in fields of silver
poly tunnels creep
towards the future while we sleep.

3.

Once a year the lord of the manor opens his gates
to the summer fete but no one sees his face.

He's always in the village
an early morning fog seeping up the lanes,

his colony of jags, his stacked-up fortune –
mostly we all bear his name, his crest is somewhere on our shelves;

we smell his perfumed breath. One day we will rebel,
the rest we swallow till our death.

4.

Witches Ladders-
Drunken Stragglers-
Ankle Biters- Scrappy Fighters-
Hairy Hand Fumblers-
Muggers-
Chuggers-
Rusty Knife Throwers-
Rough Kissers- Spiteful Lovers-
Leave you with a Pearl- Leave you with a Swell-
Leave you swearing to Merry Hell-

5.

There –
pitched on the plumes of lilac
wings flickering like a speeded-up film

of ladies in dated costumes, opening and closing parasols
If they were sound it would be
pages torn out of old-fashioned prayer books

Look! A box of junk-shop tatters
torn up carpets, Victorian borders
crimson and brackish, mottle, burnt orange

smashed at the edges with trodden-in blue glaze
white-letter, brown and purple hairstreak
silver washed and dingy, painted, copper, marbled
summer –

Clue: These all appear in the poems.

Answers: thyme (Ditch), Caravans, Earl Gray, Nettles, Butterflies.

Folklore

They said he spelled the Post Office back for an hour.
Mrs Trott bought a book of stamps,
when she got home nothing but leaves in her purse.
That's for nothing.

Squint, and up come his reedy face from the ciggy shop;
yelp and he'll stick you in his tatty bag.
He'll eat a church, he'll eat a chop, he'll make you pay.
Down in the land of Poundland, this said, oh.

He'll push you down where the stream still splutters,
throttled in the pissy trees, cut-through, once upon a time.
Cut-through, one two, one two, that's you sold to the man
come for the scraps. All gone.

That's him made up as a badger, shufty like, crosses you.
That's him as a lad late Saturday, leaking out the Camelot;
he's got you, blowing ash in your mouth, finger up there,
that's a made-up song.

The truth now, he swears,
the past, suddenly, standing up for a moment,
forgetting as it broke again upon the road,
it was no longer a small village.

Down there at the back of the old wood,
old wood what was, back of the car park now,
God bless him, back of the shop,
back of the drawer, back of beyond,

pewter what was, nettles what was,
something in the back of your throat.

Something like a small brown bird,
wren, what was, fussing with a prayer book,

down on his knees at the bus stop,
what was, pass it on. Up to his knees in it,
that old thing, thought they'd thrown it out.
Don't say he didn't warn you.

V.

Louise Warren was born and grew up in the West Country and now lives in London. With a background in theatre, her first collection *A Child's Last Picture Book of the Zoo* won the Cinnamon Press debut poetry competition and was published in 2012. A pamphlet *In the scullery with John Keats*, also published by Cinnamon, came out in 2016. Her poems have been widely published in magazines including *Ambit, The Rialto, Poetry Wales* and *Stand*. In 2018 she won first prize in the Prole Laureate Poetry Competition with her poem 'The Marshes', which appears in *John Dust*.

John Duffin is a painter and printmaker based in London. Over a 35-year career he has held over 60 one-man shows of his work and won many awards including 'Best Printmaker' award from Sir Peter Blake. His work is in many public and private collections including Museum of London, V&A, Ashmolean Oxford, Fitzwilliam Cambridge and his work was recently added to the Royal Collection of the Queen.

V.